Marketing

TIPS FOR AUTHORS

The Book Tour

ANNETTE M. MUNNICH

Stellium Books
Grant Park, Illinois 60940

Cover Art by Annette Munnich

Stellium Books
ISBN: 978-1726182089

DEDICATION

This book is dedicated to my grandchildren: Natalie, Lona, Jody, Oliver, and Nora.

Marketing Tips For Authors

INTRODUCTION

I started as a graphic artist (which is something that I still enjoy) and that has worked out well for me. I have been a graphic designer since the late 90's and have done probably thousands of promos over the years for books, radio shows, and posters... some for well-known celebrities.

In 2007, I was asked to be part of a radio show providing a ten-minute segment every week. This was fun. After a few months, the show hosts got into a dispute with the station owner and he fired everyone but me. At that point, I was offered my own radio show. Six months later I accepted the offer and started 'Python Radio' which was a paranormal talk show that lasted for four years until I stopped voluntarily.

I was using my graphic arts skills to promote my radio show heavily, which included weekly promos to announce the upcoming guests. This is how my PR career began which led to me being on staff for 2 internet-based radio stations (one in Missouri and one in New York.) I spent five years doing this. People took notice of the promos and I was being hired to produce graphics and provide some marketing and PR services.

The surprise of this was that I was being hired over and over again by authors. This began in 2009.

Consequently, I gained a unique understanding of the challenges that authors face. This includes the different positions of being with a large publisher all the way to being in the situation of independent self-publishing.

In 2014, I joined forces with a lawyer who wanted to publish books and I became the art and marketing department. After about a year I broke off on to my own publishing with the formation of Stellium Books.

I am the little guy wearing all the hats: cover design, editor, formatter, and bookkeeper. I stayed up late many nights to learn what I needed to know. Now, after three years, I also have some knowledge that only time could teach me.

Having said all of this, I have great respect and compassion for authors. Writing a book is a monumental commitment of time, energy, and discipline. Authors get criticized... brutally. Know this and continue to write anyhow.

To all of the authors here at Stellium I want you to know that I organized this information and wrote this out primarily for you. These are the different suggestions I make and I can't always remember who I told what to and if I am repeating myself. I'm sorry that I didn't do this long ago.

I almost called this book, "I wrote a book so now what???" Because that's what it is. People write books not knowing that the end is just a beginning of a new life that steps into the public eye. It's a secondary job getting the ball rolling. A job you may not have anticipated or know how to begin doing at an effective level.

So the good news and the bad news is that you successfully finished your book which is an enormous undertaking and now you have to become a salesperson.

The fantasy is that a book just totally takes off doing beautifully on Amazon and flying off of bookstore shelves. Eventually, it becomes a New York Times bestseller and we buy the house on the hill and write our next book watching the ducks swim by on our lake. It could happen and it does happen.

Our realistic goal is to have a book with steady sales and interest that is a passive income for us. I recommend that people write their books for the reason of touching lives and the satisfaction of making a lasting accomplishment that opens doors to many future possibilities.

On that note, welcome to the yellow brick road in the mysterious land of Oz and get ready to plan your book tour as large or as small as you want to make it. The book tour is your marketing and promotional plan in action with book signings, events, interviews and other ways of getting yourself and your book out there. It could be done locally only but with radio connecting you to faraway listeners and readers in places you would have never imagined. It could be more expansive and adventurous leading you to appearances and experiences in person far from your home.

The journey begins and you won't know all the places that it will lead.

May your projects be blessed.

Annette Munnich

Bradley, Illinois
July 22nd, 2018

TABLE OF CONTENTS

.

1
ENDINGS & BEGINNINGS

"We are all apprentices in a craft where no one ever becomes a master."
—Ernest Hemingway

I remember a high school reunion I attended with my boyfriend at the time for his schoolmates who were in their late fifties. During the course of the evening, they got everyone's attention and started asking questions over the microphone to the crowd of several hundred attendees. The emcee asked questions like who amongst us has climbed a mountain, been deep sea diving or lived in another country? People would then raise their hand and tell about their experiences.

One of the questions she asked was if anyone from that graduating class had authored a book.

No hands were raised. No one had written a book of any kind.

Many people talk and dream about writing a book but a surprisingly small amount of them actually do it. We may, through our interests and professions, know others who have written books personally, but on the whole, authors are still rarer than you might guess. So definitely be proud of your accomplishment.

Many authors feel like a success to complete a book and have it published. They don't need to make a million dollars or be interviewed by Oprah to feel that they accomplished something huge. After all, if the reunion was any kind of an accurate indicator, authors are rarer than deep sea divers, mountain climbers and people who have lived abroad.

On the other end of this spectrum are statistics that claim four thousand new books per day are listed on Amazon worldwide.

Yes, it is highly competitive and easy to become an obscure little fish lost in a tremendously massive ocean of books and information.

Many an author has told me that they were not prepared for what they didn't know would happen after their book came out. The thing they didn't know is that they have to participate in the marketing and publicity of their book. So many months had been spent (sometimes years) in the creation of their book that publishing was the finish line. The end. The last page, and now we just hand it over to the world and start on book two maybe.

Kind of like the books are lottery tickets and one of them might cause a windfall on their own.

Even the most prestigious publishers with books going onto shelves nationwide, or even worldwide, have their authors on a book tour of signings, appearances, radio and television interviews.

Reading all of this, you now know that you have just stepped on to the bottom rung of a new ladder in a whole new universe that you might not understand very well.

It's a little exciting, a little intimidating and a little overwhelming all at once.

The sooner that you see your book as a marketing challenge, the better off you will be on its release date.

This book is a fundamental book launching strategy. As always keep your eyes and ears open to what is working for other authors and also don't be afraid to think outside the box. I have been behind book signings and events at coffee shops, bars, historical locations, haunted houses, (real and Halloween attractions) bakeries, art galleries, metaphysical stores, tourist centers, wineries, and old theaters.

What we try to create with them is always a win/win scenario where people may show up for the event that never have been in their place of business before and become a repeat customer.

Most people coming to a book signing will look around and buy something to drink if it's available at the very least.

Your self-esteem will grow during this process. Everyone starts somewhere. Everyone that's on radio has had a first radio show. In the same regard, everyone has made mistakes on air. This applies to all in your new world of being an author. It is normal for the thought that some of these appearances feel a bit frightening.

Remember that you are there to give information about your book and give yourself credit that you are not a robot but rather an imperfect human being like the rest of us who can only do their best at the moment.

No one will remember the mistake or what color your tie or dress was. So forgive yourself in advance and step forward with your message.

Questions to ask yourself:
* ❖ What made me want to write this book?
* ❖ In a few short sentences, what is my book about?
* ❖ What were your challenges in writing it?
* ❖ If your book has a message what is it?
* ❖ Did anyone inspire the creation of your idea and/or book?

❖ Are you aspiring to write more books, and if yes, why and what genres?
❖ What kind of books do you like reading and why?
❖ What authors left a lasting impact on you?

You are now prepared for an interview.

Please write a short description of your book as well as a medium length and longer version. For the long version do not go longer than one page. This is for confidence and clarity in relaying what your book is about and you won't have to think of a way to describe it on the spot. You will know what to say and you will say it with confidence.

Be prepared to discuss aspects of your book in depth without giving away spoilers or so much information that it doesn't seem intriguing to purchase and read it all in its entirety.

2
THREE WAYS TO MAKE MONEY

"Books are a uniquely portable magic."
— Stephen King, On Writing: A Memoir of the Craft

There are three ways to make money with your book.

The first way to make money from your book is most obvious and that is royalties from sales on Amazon and other online platforms, plus retailers. A passive income is a beautiful thing, and a book you wrote this year can still be earning some money for you while you are writing another book or taking a nap three years from now.

Some books are released and Amazon customers respond in a large enough and consistent enough way to keep a book visible on the bestseller and hot new release lists for months. This is, of course, what we are all hoping for. In my opinion, nothing is as helpful to a book as its visibility on Amazon to readers browsing for books in that genre.

In truth, the most common scenario is that the book makes a little splash in the beginning and then begins to slide off of these lists altogether. I have had books stay top ten and top twenty for six months or more. I wish they all did. A lot of thought and analysis goes into the development of the cover, description, blurb, genres and even timing of availability to the public. All of this is in the hopes of the book holding a position of accomplishment and high visibility on Amazon for as long as possible.

Most of our books at Stellium get picked up by Barnes and Noble and Books a Million online. This is online only on their websites and does not mean the book is on store shelves nationally.

The second way to make money from your book is from the copies the author buys at a huge discount and then sells at events and/or through their website. The website copies are signed and don't forget to charge a shipping fee.

Most of the authors at Stellium do very well at events. The pricing will be up to you. I recommend sticking with a rounded number and not accepting checks. You can go to PayPal and get an attachment for your phone that scans debit and credit cards. PayPal is also the best way to accept money through your website and they do convert world currencies for you if you decide to accept orders from other countries.

The third way to make money from your book is using it as a draw to your existing business or profession, with the book expanding your reach and giving you credibility.

You could also start a business or offer services connected to the subject matter of your book.

You might also lecture and/or conduct workshops on your topic or even on writing itself, and the book is your product being sold at the back of the room.

3

IMMEDIATE AUTHOR BENEFITS

"People don't realize how a man's whole life can be changed by one book."
— Malcolm X

As of day one, your book release date, you have gained a voice in the world and a measure of respect. You did what a lot of people say they want to do, but ended up watching TV instead. This shows dedication and everyone knows that. It also shows courage. Some people finish a book and never get the nerve to have it published due to fear of rejection and feeling so exposed. Some don't have enough faith in their writing skills and feel unworthy.

If what you wrote about is connected to your business or service you can be instantly seen as a leader in your field. Cutting edge... Mover and shaker... Your head and shoulders above your peers, competitors, and colleagues.

You may not be a famous person but you have taken a step into the public eye. You will be admired and also criticized. Your opinions and commentary may be asked for.

In reality, when a book goes out into the world we don't have any clue how far it can go and into whose hands. We don't know if it will cause a reaction or not. It's your words let loose into the universe.

If you do have a business or service your book is being read by your customers and your readers are finding your business. It can be a very lovely thing.

Along the way, you will most likely be pleasantly surprised at some of the heartfelt feedback and touching reviews you receive... and some of it from far away places that blow your mind. Getting an e-mail from someone in Japan or India is quite a thrill.

Maybe in a small way you are making a difference. Your life is, in return, enriched by your readers.

You are a member of a select group of people who organized their thoughts and made a commitment to your words and decided you had enough confidence to step out under a spotlight and sometimes microscope.

Be proud of yourself. In your own way, you opened a door of possibilities to a much bigger life.

4

HOW PUBLISHERS THINK

"I guess there are never enough books."
— John Steinbeck, A John Steinbeck Encyclopedia

First, let's look at how authors think.

❖ I wrote my life story and I've always wanted to do that.

❖ My book is so beautifully written that they can't help but be impressed.

❖ I even designed my own cover from a picture that means a lot to me.

In short, you may have written a book about yourself for yourself and just assume it will mean something to someone else.

Having said that, a lot of people have remarkable stories and insights and I do publish them and they do sell.

Just like any form of art you have to get the attention of the reader and touch them emotionally or else it won't work. Read that sentence twice.

Now you give your book to a publisher or literary agent and if it doesn't get accepted you might assume it's poorly written when the probable truth is that they don't find it to be remarkable and also marketable.

How Publishers Think
- ❖ How well are current books of this type selling?
- ❖ How is this book competitive and appealing in that genre?
- ❖ What are the demographics of its audience?
- ❖ Do we generally make money or lose money on books of this type?

All of that was on the table before your actual writing was focused on.

Your book is a product that they risk losing time and money on.

Major publishers order a first printing and books are shipped to retailers. This is an investment and they are being asked to invest in you.

If your book doesn't perform well sales-wise it eventually ends up in the Dollar Store and they swallow the loss. Too many bad losses in a year and their business suffers.

If you are interviewed by a publisher you may get asked this question, "In what way is your book different from other books in this genre?" When you answer that say something to the effect of "I have endeavored to take this to another level." On the one hand, it seems a lot of effort made by them to look for new and unusual things but actually, it's kind of a lot like movies and television. On TV a certain kind of show will be popular and a lot more like it will be produced. When I was a kid there would be times where it was crime dramas, westerns, medical dramas, etc.

That was a long time ago but what is never a long time ago is the reality of current trends. What are people concerned with and responding to at the moment?

So while it may seem like everyone is waiting for something new and different, if something is hot and selling right now, your book in that genre, if well written, could be a safer bet.

Children's book authors might go on Amazon and see that the majority of the top 20 bestsellers are about dogs. Due to this, they may think it's brilliant to go the other way and do cats. But, it's possible that there is a new cartoon out or Disney movie about dogs and that is pushing the trend and you don't see that and you miss it.

Of course, you should write the books waiting to be written in your heart. Having said that, maybe write one for an attempt at mass current appeal with all of your other titles listed at the end of it to breathe new life into the writing you already have out there.

Major publishers may decide in advance that they will only release three western books this year because the genre is not popular at this time. So if you have a western the competition may be stiff and you don't even know it.

As an art based person, I like to believe that everything that is truly magnificent gets its chance to be seen and appreciated.

Publishing is a highly speculative and highly competitive field. Huge gains possible and huge losses... I have a huge advantage in being a little guy in the publishing world working with print on demand instead of huge initial printing orders and my overhead is low. I can weather whatever happens with a book pretty well without having to feel panic about going under due to poor sales and risk-taking. I will say that a lot of thought goes into the presentation of each book in regard to the cover, description, layout etc... and it is depressing sometimes to miss the mark in spite of best efforts.

Books are very much like TV and Movies with floods of what has been selling being offered to the public over and over until the next trend comes in and the original one slows down. If I might be very bold I would go ahead and say that that comes before everything, even, and most especially, quality content.

Most, if not all, major publishers do **not** accept unsolicited manuscripts so a literary agent is necessary. Normally, they have some ideas of what they are looking for and have scouts finding books that meet those criteria.

5
KNOW YOUR AUDIENCE

"We write to taste life twice, in the moment and in retrospect."
— Anaïs Nin

Television knows its audience well and if you pay attention to all of the commercials and add them up they will tell you who they think are watching that program. This is how Soap Operas got to be called Soap Operas as they were literally selling soap and other homemaker items of interest to married women during the day. When I am watching World War Two shows on the History Channel through the commercials I see that they think I am an older man with back pain.

I publish paranormal, spiritual, and metaphysical books among other things, but I started heavily in this genre. I bring it up because these books have a demographic that could literally be anyone. Both sexes of any background and age can likely be a reader if they find the subject matter interesting. This book that I am writing now is similar in having a universal appeal if the reader has an interest in the information.

In the case of children's books, especially, know what age group you have written for and keep inside of the perimeter of their vocabulary. The age group the book falls into should be in the book description.

If your book does have a specific audience, then that is where your marketing efforts primarily go and this includes the look and "feel" of your blog, website... etc.

Know your audience, and notice what they are responding to, in general.

One of the authors I publish, for example, started a blog from my suggestion, and it was baby blue with a floral accent. She is the author of one of the creepiest books I have published so far. The website looked like she was about to share brownie recipes.

Sometimes authors give me photos to use to create the cover of their book and the images are of things they like or are important to them for one reason or another. Sometimes the covers are already started by an author who thinks he or she understands what they want their book to look like. That's the way it is approached instead of looking at other covers that are currently selling in that genre and pursuing the development of a cover that has the right "feel" to it.

Your cover is the first thing connecting your reader's eyes to you and your words. So who is your cover for?

Know your audience.

6
PIC, BIO, POSTER, & BOOK SHEET

"There is no greater agony than bearing an untold story inside you."
— Maya Angelou, I Know Why the Caged Bird Sings

Let's dive into some of your basic promotional necessities. If you don't have these in place, especially the first two, you will be asked for them and be empty-handed. Any radio show, newspaper, magazine, any kind of media, will ask for your pic and bio.

While you do need a professional looking photo, you do not need to pay a professional photographer for their services. A good quality phone camera and a friend with some patience can get good results.

A headshot is what you need not a full or half body picture. Look towards the light for a flattering image without shadows on your face. Outdoor photos are very nice. Having the final pic converted to black and white can look very sharp.

Be patient and don't be hard on yourself during the process of picture taking. It's possible that you might like only one or two out of ten or twelve attempts.

The background should be plain. A brick or stone wall is nice, or just a painted wall. Simple greenery, if outside, is good. No telephone poles looking like they are growing out of your head... Look at the background too when taking photos and you can get some quality looking photographs.

Take the photos in a large size and e-mail them to yourself. They can always be sized down for whatever you may need, but the large size makes nice clear posters. If you have a photo editing program you can crop them and make a black and white version. Square photos go well on back covers.

This is the lovely Jacqueline Davieau in a very natural and flattering pose in black and white with her name added.

Sometimes I do use full body photos for posters. Rick Kueber in his promo poster for "The Convergence Saga." I use artificial backgrounds.

Cole Collins' promo poster for "The Witch of Washington." The artificial background mimics the book cover.

The reason that a poster is a good idea is because it can be printed and used for book signings and events. It can also be used to have a huge vinyl banner made and you can use it on social media as well.

Elements of a book poster include:
- ❖ Book cover image
- ❖ Where the book can be found such as Amazon etc... use logos.
- ❖ Author pic and name
- ❖ Publisher name
- ❖ Release date
- ❖ Short description can be added.
- ❖ For ease of printing make 8.5 by 11 size or 850 by 1100 pixels.

One of the authors printed out some at regular copy paper size and had them laminated so they can be used multiple times and it looks good on bookstore doors or windows.

Any type of media will ask for your pic and bio. When you create your bio the trend lately is to be friendly and whimsical and say things like... so and so likes rainy Sunday afternoons sipping latte with her calico cat Matilda. A little bit of that is okay I guess, but mainly that's not what people are looking for.

Things to include in your bio:
- ❖ Where you are from/ birthplace

- ❖ Other books you have written
- ❖ Media appearances
- ❖ Your professions/ education
- ❖ Your experience concerning the book subject matter.
- ❖ Special interests/ hobbies (optional)
- ❖ Family information (optional)

If you have an extensive background it's good to have a shorter and longer version (no more than two pages.) It is professional to have a media kit (also called press kit) if you have a lot to list, with a page for your background, one for your other books and one for your media appearances with photos they can use and of course your contact information on first and last pages.

The book sheet has your book information on it and how you can be contacted. It is primarily for bookstores and libraries. The book title goes on top of the page with the author's name below that. Have your book cover image at the top of the page. List the book's ISBN number, publisher (if applicable), release date, dimensions, genres (BISAC code) and page count. Any accomplishments the book has should be under the title and author name before the details. Example: Number one best seller in Supernatural on Amazon

The middle paragraph is book description or use the back cover blurb.

The last paragraph lists other books from the author and contact information. The stores order your books through the ISBN number. Your contact info is in case they have questions or would like you to come for an appearance/ book signing. Hyperlink the title and book image to your book's page on Amazon.

UNDER. ATTACK.

Deepest Darkest Secrets Revealed

Katie N. McHale

#1 Hot New Release Amazon Supernatural
Best-Seller in Supernatural Amazon 6/2018

6" x 9" (15.24 x 22.86 cm)
Black & White on White paper
228 pages
ISBN-13: 978-1720978640 Stellium Books
ISBN-10: 1720978646
BISAC: Body, Mind & Spirit / Supernatural
A VERY RAW ACCOUNT OF DEMONIC OPPRESSION AND ATTACHMENT THAT LED TO POSSESSION AND FINALLY... EXORCISM

A real case of deliverance from evil with the 'Spiritual Warrior' Bill Bean.

One woman's brave journey that started in her family home which has been haunted for generations. She endures sexual abuse

Screenshot of book sheet for Katie McHale "Under Attack." Displaying top half only.

Having these four things in place will be very handy and additionally, some authors invest in FB headers, vinyl banners, bookmarks and/or rack cards. I suggest rack cards as they are somewhat bigger and serve the same purpose as the bookmarks. We have more space on them to use. Business cards are good to have as well.

7
REVIEWS & RECOMMENDATIONS

"And by the way, everything in life is writable about if you have the outgoing guts to do it, and the imagination to improvise. The worst enemy to creativity is self-doubt."
— Sylvia Plath, The Unabridged Journals of Sylvia Plath

Ugh, reviews. It seems like readers want to tell you how much they enjoyed your book and how much it meant to them one on one, but they don't put it on Amazon where it helps. If you like a book, leave a review and star rating on Amazon for the authors. Don't quote me on this, but I believe the number of reviews you need for Amazon to really help promote your book is 50. All that really needs to be said is... this book is a great read.

Getting reviews and recommendations in advance of the book release can be done through sharing a non-editable PDF if they are willing to read a digital version. I'm in a situation right now where we plan on releasing the book on Amazon just long enough for us to get some copies sent to the author so he can distribute them to notable people he knows in his field. The cover will be updated after that with the good reviews on the back cover and maybe a short one on the front. Then we will make the book available to the public again.

The reviews can be listed inside the book as well.

Good reviews help a lot and a review by someone considered to be an "expert" in your book's genre can make a difference.

You can also have a good review added into the book description, put on the book sheet or poster.

Critical reviews from book experts can help or break a book if they trash you on your skills.

If you find a website connected to the type of book you wrote you might offer that person the chance to read you for free and recommend the book to the page followers if the response is favorable.

Some people will nitpick you and your book. Sometimes they even ridicule the subject which makes me wonder why they read it. Have a thick skin and discern what is helpful criticism from what is not. We are all evolving as writers, publishers, and individuals. So it's part of the journey. Something about you struck enough of a cord for them to bother themselves to write something about the book.

8
MEDIA (TV RADIO NEWSPAPERS)

"No tears in the writer, no tears in the reader. No surprise in the writer, no surprise in the reader."
— Robert Frost

Before you get discouraged about approaching big media platforms such as TV, newspapers, or radio, take a moment to consider that these outlets are on a constant quest for interesting content.

I'll start with newspapers to begin this chapter.

Unfortunately, newspapers are becoming more of a dinosaur with every passing day and most of the subscribers are older people. The internet has changed everything.

In smaller areas, getting an interview (or a review) is less difficult. In larger cities, it's harder, but the good news is that papers in large cities are still being heavily read by commuters on a daily basis.

How to approach a newspaper:
- ❖ Look at your local paper for a book section, which may appear only on Sundays

- ❖ Secondarily you might find an Arts & Humanities section in the Sunday paper
- ❖ Thirdly, Culture and Community.
- ❖ Take note of the journalist's names on the articles.
- ❖ You can usually find contact information for the journalists on the newspaper website.
- ❖ You can write a letter to the editor and often they will assign the story to one of their writers if they are interested.

Signing up to receive email notifications at www.helpareporter.com can be useful. 'HARO' connects journalists to "experts" that they need in order to have sources and sometimes interviews for their assignments etc... You will need to watch for these emails and respond quickly.

The best avenue for local television is through the early morning news/talk programs. They will be called Good Day or Good Morning whatever town you are in, or something similar. You can find a contact form on their website. I have done these before using FAX as well and they were very responsive.

Radio interviews come in two varieties. The first consists of the standard fare on your local radio dial. This is what we all have grown up with and even though there was a time where radios were in homes, people mostly are listening in their cars only at this point in time. You will need to contact each show you are interested in through the show's producers. Find the information on their website.

The second type of radio interview is through internet radio stations and recorded podcasts. These opportunities are plentiful. Blogtalk Radio is a huge platform where you can find shows on a huge variety of topics so it's a good place to search for prospects.

Another good resource for interview opportunities is called Radio Guest List. Sign up on their website for notifications of shows looking for guests. This site handles both kinds of radio shows. I have found some very good opportunities by using it. radioguestlist.com

In your approach letter for local media I often start with the subject matter with "Do You Support Local Authors?" in the subject line followed by what kind of show it would be, such as "Vegan Cooking." These people are very busy and will ask for more details if interested so don't send a lengthy e-mail.

Sample e-mail:
Subject line
Do You Support Local Authors? "High School Football"

Hello,

If you and your audience might be interested in a fun and informative show about High School Football, I would love to be a guest. My new book, "Playing High School Football: Keys To Your Success" was a #1 Hot New Release on Amazon and a best seller in Coaching genre. I am a seasoned guest and comfortable with call-in questions.
Add link to your book on Amazon next.
Thank you for your time.

That simple e-mail can get you a lot of responses. Customize for your own purposes. Shorter is better and just like knowing your audience in readers, know your audience when pitching. Radio and television programs want to know what the subject for the show is and what information you have to offer on the topic. They also worry that people are "bad" guests who will clam up and get nervous with a lot of dead air time so if you are experienced let them know that as well. You can add a bullet list of what kind of information your book offers. Your goal is selling books but their goal is a good show.

Have your pic and bio ready.

9
ARTICLE WRITING AND BLOGGING

"You must stay drunk on writing so reality cannot destroy you."
— Ray Bradbury, Zen in the Art of Writing

Writing articles is another way to reach people interested in your topic by way of participating in established platforms. A good article for submission will be at least 600 words. Inquiring magazines on and offline should give you access to their individual 'specs' (specifications) for submissions and publication. Some platforms will run longer articles while some others view space as a premium so you need to find out before you send over 1600 words.

The second thing with writing for magazines is that it is standard for them to want exclusive rights to the article you've provided. Sometimes this is for a set period of time like 6 months or one year, but sometimes it's forever.

You will not be paid unless you have been invited to write as a regular contributor and even then, for online mags you may not be offered financial compensation.

The benefit to you is getting your name out there to a new crowd of potential followers and book buyers. Normally a very short bio is presented and your book or books listed after your name.

I have written for magazines as well as many of the authors here at Stellium. Currently, we have one author on staff writing articles for a magazine regularly. It's a good way to get out there with some exposure in your writing field and looks <u>very</u> good in your bio.

Blogging is essentially articles or even an online journal that you are writing for your own page. Wordpress is a good place to start a blog for free and it isn't hard to set up and design the look. Many people browse the new articles at Wordpress in the genres they have interest in.

Be mindful when naming your blog as just naming the blog your name doesn't offer readers much of a clue as to what this page is about. Or incorporate a meaning into the title with your name such as 'Organic Gardening' with Mary Kay etc...

Design your blog to look like your subject matter. A slick, all black background with modern touches does not provide a complimentary 'home' for Mary Kay's Organic Gardening, even if she thinks that looks cool. Okay, so again, it's about drawing the attention of the readers.

To set up your Wordpress blog, go to www.wordpress.com and sign up to create a free site. Have all of your blog posts appear on your homepage. Don't make the reader have to look around to find your articles/posts. Have an 'About Me' page with your bio and pic. Make a book page with your book description, cover image, and link to the book on Amazon. Of course, have a 'Contact Me' page as well. These four pages set you up for a very basic but effective site.

The most important feature on your homepage is the 'Follow Me' which we need to be up near the top on the right-hand side. We want them to enter their e-mail addy here so they are informed of all future posts when they go live.

It used to be that you could link to your social media pages and the posts you make would automatically show up on all of them, but Facebook is changing this and you will have to take your post links onto Facebook to submit manually. To my knowledge, we will still be able to use the automatic post on LinkedIn and Twitter. It's a nice option for the writers.

Speaking of Facebook, if you have a Facebook page for your book or yourself as an author, you can have a spot on your home page for people to connect with it.

Sharing excerpts is fine as well as talking about writing and the creative process itself, your topic or genre, and what you are writing now.

I choose Wordpress because of the number of readers they have and ease of setting up a site, but these tips will help you on another blog site if you choose something different to use.

10
BOOK SIGNINGS

"There is no real ending. It's just the place where you stop the story."
— Frank Herbert

Book signings are a lot of fun and a good way to build a following in your area. If you know that you will be traveling it's a nice idea to set up a book signing in that area as well. Why not meet people interested in your books all around the country and even possibly beyond our borders? So if you're going to see your Aunt Betty in Wichita, line up a book signing and now it becomes a business trip with deductible expenses.

Most obviously we have book signings in bookstores but feel free to think outside the box on this. Authors I have worked with and my own authors here at Stellium have had book events at wineries, haunted house attractions, tourist information centers, coffee shops, historical sites, metaphysical stores art galleries, old theaters, and bakeries.

Very good locations include anything in a downtown city area, airport and train station stores, historical and cultural popular attractions. In other words, places where a lot of foot traffic exists.

Some of the unusual places you may approach might never have had a book signing before and could be uninterested and dismissive. Others may have a broader entrepreneurial outlook and think it's a cool idea and why not?

Some locations may have a room they rent out for events and try to sell you on that but don't get talked into room rental fees. In fact, unless you want to book a speaking engagement that party room is worse than having a small table visible from the front door entrance.

What you need for a book signing:
- ❖ Your poster and at least two weeks of it being displayed at the location prominently (front door, window, or cash register)
- ❖ Table and chair visible from the main entrance
- ❖ 2 hours is a good allotment of time
- ❖ 15-24 books is usually good
- ❖ Business cards and/or rack cards
- ❖ Table sign of some kind or banner across table front.
- ❖ A Pen
- ❖ A PayPal swipe that attaches to your phone for accepting debit and credit

cards or you will be stuck accepting cash only.

❖ Make the book price a rounded number for easy cash payment and not needing to have a lot of coins to make change.

Calling is better than email when approaching a business. Try not to call during their busiest time of day if it's obvious, for example, coffee shops during morning hours etc... Facebook business pages usually give good responses too and the advantage here is that they can quickly see who you are.

In your approach ask for the owner, manager, or person who sets up events. Tell them you are a local author and you would love (not like) to have a book signing at their establishment and will provide advertising materials plus you will advertise locally and through social media.

If they ask why you are interested in their location explain that you enjoy meeting people in the community from all walks of life.

Coffee shops and wineries are not hard to get because they realize that the people who come will buy a beverage almost guaranteed.

Do your best to be friendly and make a win/win scenario without being pushy. A no from them is a no, and cross them off your list and continue. Don't feel bad about any no you get because it isn't a rejection of you as much as an inability on their end to do something unconventional more times than not. You are a potential avenue for fresh customers to find them and become repeat business sales.

Smaller bookstores are normally very agreeable to this and used to having authors in for events. Used bookstores sometimes don't do it.

Books A Million has been easier to deal with, for me in my own experiences, than **Barnes And Noble**. Barnes seems to have a lot of retail stores in their chain with independent decision making and some B & N stores won't do book events anymore at all or they might have you at one of their author fairs where they have multiple authors coming in and those are nice. At Barnes, you have to deal directly with the event coordinator and no one else in that store can or will help you. One B & N asked me to submit my advertising plan for the event in writing with a promise that at least 75 people will come.

Having said all of that, some Barnes and Noble stores are very supportive of local authors and enjoy having these events plus speaking engagements and also provide a local author's shelf and will keep your books in stock and on display. You don't know until you call.

It's important to understand the agreement you are walking into with the bookstores. Most will order your book and stock whatever isn't sold on the shelves, which is good as your foot is in the door and when they sell the leftover books they often will place an order for more and you are now in their inventory. That day, however, you won't make any money, unlike the coffee shop where you brought the books that you bought wholesale and sold them for retail pocketing the profits.

I have had smaller bookstores ask the authors to bring books with them but then wanted a cut from the sales that day. If you do a deal with this person even though he is taking some of the money he is also interested in the success of the event and will be promoting it as hard as you do and not all of the bookstores do that.

Advertise your book signing locally by using the free papers (that come to everyone's mail... ours is Country Market) city, town and county websites (upcoming events page) and Craigslist allows event postings.

Libraries also have book events and events where the authors read to children but are normally adverse to anyone selling a book at these times.

11
PITCHING TO RETAILERS

"Start writing, no matter what. The water does not flow until the faucet is turned on."
— Louis L'Amour

Bookstores overall don't do as well as they used to. Being from Chicago I can recall many happy afternoons in Kroch's and Brentano's and Waldenbooks. Now neither of those chains exist. Waldenbooks was owned by Border's and that chain is gone too.

A pitch for your book to a large book retailer needs to be sent via conventional mail for best results. This can be your book page and bio along with media appearances (if any) and a formal letter to that company.

They require a book to have the price listed on the back in US and Canadian currencies plus a bar code.

Barnes And Noble and Books A Million have scouts that pick up your book and offer it for sale on their online websites. This does not mean that your book is on their store shelves because it doesn't mean that it is and it also doesn't mean that you will necessarily have an easier time pitching them to be in their stores nationwide. This also doesn't mean that they bought a pile of your books. If someone orders they will order one of your books at retailer price and sell it for list price. So, it's free for them to be a middleman and why not?

It is exciting to be chosen and included.

Books A Million is notorious for failing to respond at all to pitching. Barnes And Noble is better about responding and even if they don't pick a title up for nationwide inclusion in their stores they have options for local and also regional inclusion.

I have had authors get responses from Walmart corporate offices.

Nicer truck stops carry books and many truck drivers spend some downtime reading. Pilot responds to pitches.

Smaller stores you can pitch at the same time as you approach about possible book signings.

Where else could you pitch your book? Depending on genre, places like metaphysical stores, sporting goods stores, hospital gift shops and more may be options. Don't forget the library!

12
LOCAL AUTHOR EVENTS & GROUPS

"History will be kind to me for I intend to write it."
— Winston S. Churchill

Local author groups can be fun and bring nice opportunities your way. One of my best friends is in an active one that does projects together and hosts some annual events.

I see an attitude of competition sometimes with authors. Personally, I like to encounter successful people as they are our mentors and show us not only how it's done but that it **can** be done.

Google the name of your city with the word "authors" to find out what is going on in your area. Meetup.com is a nice site to search on or if you want to start a group. www.meetup.com

Author events are sometimes teamed up with arts and crafts vendors. Also, all of your local town events can be a good place for you to have a table and be in the community selling books and meeting people. Some author's groups hold events in church halls and even combine it with their Christmas Bazaar.

Some author events are very high dollar and prestigious. You will not be able to sell enough books to recover the cost of the table but it has its own benefits in networking and exposure. These are mainly in the larger cities and downtown areas.

Another kind of author event or expo features authors and has a speaker schedule on topics connected to books and writing. These are nice and sometimes last entire weekends. When they are large enough, they are often found at hotels to accommodate authors, speakers, and attendees from out of town.

Combine an author event with a fundraiser at a local charity or historical site.

If you want to start setting up your own local events find a venue willing to do an inexpensive or free win/win situation with you and be patient. The first year may be a small turnout. It can take a while to build this into a sizeable annual event, so keep the costs down.

13

SPEAKING ENGAGEMENTS WORKSHOPS & WEBINARS

"There is something delicious about writing the first words of a story. You never quite know where they'll take you."
— Beatrix Potter

Non-Fiction books can often easily turn into opportunities for speaking engagements, workshops, webinars and online courses.

Webinars and online courses can be exciting and highly effective for book sales, building an e-mail list, exposure and even one on one coaching. Sometimes what we are actually doing is having the course or webinar as a marketing tool from idea conception and each book chapter is the topic for the weekly lesson or webinar.

Yes, and you get their e-mail addys when they sign up for the free webinar with the book for sale and private coaching at the end if applicable.

The downside is that this takes a lot of preparation and work but the upside is that webinars and courses can be used again and again as long as your information is relevant.

Do you love this yet? You should.

… And you are helping people learn and improve themselves and their lives. Stand up and do it. Good for you. Once the first one is finished start planning the second and you must work on keeping up to date in your field.

For online courses, you may like Udemy www.udemy.com. Metaphysical and self-improvement courses do well on Daily Om www.dailyom.com

Most of the webinars I attend (and I have attended a lot) are on Citrix.com but you are free to search for others to try out. www.citrix.com

Workshops are invigorating and lovely in person. I do like the application on a grander scale to becoming online events. Do you have a workbook or journal? Can you create one?

You truly can create so many good things this way for yourself and others. There may be a small voice in your head that says "Who am I to do this?" I know that voice well. It definitely has been the information age for a long time now so don't take your knowledge and experience for granted.

Speaking engagements are awesome if it doesn't scare you. Let what you have to say be followed by a Q&A. All we can do is our best at the moment.

One of my first clients back in 2009 was with a publisher that went out of business and she went on a mission to buy all the copies they had printed of her book. So she had boxes and boxes of her book in her garage and lived in a remote location.

She is in the genre of pets which is enormously popular and we built the price of the book into the ticket so that every attendee received a book to take home after her lecture.

I don't get into scrapes like this as I am print on demand which keeps my overhead down and makes sense for me. I am very low overhead so if one book doesn't perform I can wait it out until the next one does.

I love historic theaters, locations, and universities as venues for speaking engagements. Be sure to have someone reliable and meticulous record it on video. To not do so is a huge waste. The lecture in clips or in its entirety can be used as a promo on your website, YouTube, and various social media as well as a boost in your pitching efforts.

Connectedness is key. How does one thing affect and or lead to another?

Over the course of your writing career you may end up with numerous books and each one regenerates the subsequent ones. Of course, your other books are listed in your new book and links are also provided to help Kindle readers continue reading.

Normally with speaking engagements, you will need a friend to sit at a table in the back of the room selling your books and compiling a list of people wanting signatures. Have business cards and/or rack cards available with your website, blog, and e-mail but not phone.

14
SOCIAL MEDIA

"You can make anything by writing."
— C.S. Lewis

Do you need social media? Yes. Can you rely on it for steady sales? No.

I'm going to tell your ego something it doesn't want to hear. You are seen as interesting and influential and maybe even cute. People follow you who have no intention of reading your book although they will lie and say they will to obtain your friendship. They don't know that you can know this.

Most of the book sales come within the first 2 weeks to a month after the book's release date and then spotty here and there after that.

It's good to make a page for your book or yourself as an author and grow that over time.

Advertising your new book every single day is a lot and can become irritating to your friends and followers. There are book groups that authors advertise on so joining a few of those can be helpful.

Combining efforts with another author is nice and you both advertise for each other.

I like LinkedIn and Pinterest. Many of the authors have Twitter accounts. Twitter and Facebook are the standards I think, although, I do not Snap Chat or Instagram.

Some people hire a social media manager as it gets to be a lot of work and time involved. In this day and age, you almost have to do it to some extent.

If you are busy and/or actively writing it's not a great idea to connect your phone to Facebook unless you really don't mind your phone beeping with notifications and messages all day long. I use mine through my laptop.

Even if you have a lot of friends and connections social media is not enough to keep sales going strong so it's best not to have that expectation.

We have used paid ads on FB with mixed results. Careful analysis was applied and sometimes two ads were used to see which one was better. The results are often surprising and variable. It's worth trying and running an ad from time to time.

15

AMAZON STATS, AUTHOR PAGE, AND ADS

"Cut out all these exclamation points. An exclamation point is like laughing at your own joke."
— F. Scott Fitzgerald

Amazon stats update hourly. So the bestseller lists are always in a state of flux according to the sales happening at the moment. We have had several Stellium titles achieve number one status in their genre. The top book we've had bounced around the top three for five months.

In addition to the bestseller lists, there are lists for Hot New Releases in all genres.

On your book's Amazon page it shows the different formats available for your book such as; paperback, hardcover, Kindle or audiobook. Each of these formats has its own stats. Your book could be number five bestseller in your genre for Kindle and number ten in paperback. Simultaneously, it can be number one hot new release.

So we will imagine now that we clicked on the Kindle format to look at our Kindle stats. Scroll down the page a bit until you see a section called product details. Your book information will be listed there as well as your book's current rank. A rank of under 30,000 is damn good. Remember that your standings are changing by the hour. If your book doesn't sell every day it will be hard to hold a good rank. There are 4 possible scenarios with books. There are the books that come out strong and perform well over time as the customers that look for books in that genre on Amazon are buying it steadily. There are books that sell in the very beginning and then slide but are steady sellers on a lesser level. There are books that make a splash initially from an interest in the release and then drop off to probably not return to the bestseller list again. The last kind of book doesn't make rank from the start and seems destined for obscurity in spite of your best efforts.

Under the rank, you will find it's numerical rank in its genre(s) If it isn't under the number 100 the book is not on the best seller list in that category. The higher the number, the farther the book is from being a bestseller. You will find that the genre title is clickable and that will take you to the bestseller page for that genre.

If your book has been doing very well, check this page often. You will find the way to view the hot new releases in the same category from the bestseller page.

Here is Stellium Book's Amazing Paranormal Encounters Volumes 1 and 2 holding the number 1 and number 3 spots on Amazon Unexplained Mysteries bestseller list.

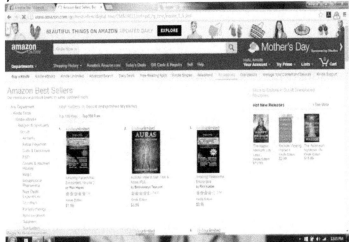

Here we are coming in at number 2 across the board 6 months after release. Amazing Paranormal Encounters Volume 1 was a top 3 spot holder for a year.

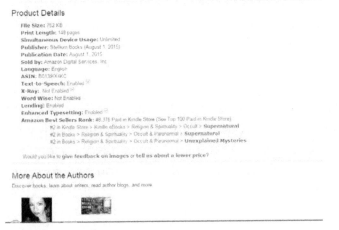

The funny thing is that Amazing Paranormal Encounters Volumes 1 and 2 plus Rick Kueber's Forever Ash, did so well for us as first books that I thought it was easy to make books that totally dominated the bestseller lists. Even though Stellium still did well I had a few rude awakenings with books that did not perform and started to realize the huge accomplishments we made from the very start.

Another way to check your book's performance is by making an Amazon Author Page and you should definitely have one because people find you here with your bio, pic and all of your books.

On your Amazon Author Page, you will be able to track your sales and know if they are going up or down.

I am amazed at how many authors don't know this stuff. The consequences of not knowing are continuing a lot of paid and free promotional efforts without knowing if they work at all. I've seen authors having fantasies about big royalty checks coming when they don't actually have a clue if they sold 10 books, 100 books or a thousand... A lot of radio shows claim to have a big audience, but if you watch your stats you will find out which ones have a sizeable audience of potential readers for you and your type of book.

Go to Amazon Author Central to find the link to make your page. authorcentral.amazon.com

Amazon has some promotional options that you can access yourself if you are self-publishing through your KDP page or through your publisher. The first thing they offer is 6 days every quarter where you can give your Kindle away for free. Some publishers may say no to this but it can be a decent move for a few reasons. I especially like it for an author with more than one book as letting readers have the first for free can lead them to purchase the second and etc... Getting a book some visibility via the free pages can be helpful. People can follow your blog and plug into what you are doing. I have some authors who have written books to help people and generously offer them for free from time to time for that reason alone.

Amazon paid ads (again through KDP) are ads shown on Kindles to readers that buy books similar to yours. It's a pay per click system and I recommend you watch it as the ad in larger genres can get pricey if it isn't converting into sales. I have done okay with these. There is a small amount of text that is allowed so put some thought into how you want to draw readers into your book. You won't be allowed more than a few lines with the image of your book cover.

16
BOOK LAUNCH PARTIES

"You can't wait for inspiration. You have to go after it with a club."
— Jack London

Not everyone chooses to do this but it's nice and a very cool way to start your promotional efforts. Sometimes these events can be newspaper-worthy as a story in a smaller area. They can be open to the public and advertised well in advance.

The author will have a stack of books just like a book signing.

Appetizers are nice to serve and cake is good. We got one made with the book cover image on it (done beautifully) by, believe it or not, Walmart, and not for a bad price either.

Honestly, the sky is the limit on creating your party and it can be simple, lasting only a few hours on a Sunday afternoon, or a much more elaborate affair with cocktails and music.

I always feel that inviting people with a personal touch is many times more effective than something like creating a Facebook event even if it's public and all are welcome.

This needs to be planned about a month in advance to get the word out properly and be careful being too close to your actual release date in case any delays cause you to not have books with you which is not the idea at all of course.

Take lots of photos of the event and at least a few of you sitting at a table with your books. These pics make great promo pics for all kinds of things in the future.

Intriguing historical sites are so cool for these types of parties. Have a print out with interesting facts on the location and people wander around taking a look and have something to talk about besides the book.

Libraries often have a room that can be used with permission.

I stay away from outdoor plans as it saves me weeks of worrying about the weather prior to events but they can be fabulous when it works out well.

Don't create something so complicated that it takes away from your ability to be truly happy and having your attention on the guests. Simple and a little elegant, vintage, or whimsical is a great theme.

17
UPDATE ACCOMPLISHMENTS

"If my doctor told me I had only six minutes to live, I wouldn't brood. I'd type a little faster."
— Isaac Asimov

You need to update your bio at least once a year. More often if important things are happening. Make new promos. Take your accomplishments with you.

These stats are a few years old but 4 thousand new books are released on Amazon every single day. It's so very easy to just be an obscure little fishy lost in the vast ocean of books that is Amazon.

If you made a mark and people paid attention to you and what you wrote for even a short time that is a job well done.

So if you made number 1 hot new release in your genre, or better yet, the best seller list that's wonderful. The higher on the list the better and the longer on the list the better, obviously. Top 20 and higher is very nice. So forever you can say bestseller on Amazon in whatever genre. Let them know it's that and not the NY Times bestseller list.

Some genres are smaller and easier to dominate than others but that also means fewer pairs of eyes are seeing the book.

If you get invited to a well-known radio or television program list that as well as any articles you wrote for magazines, speaking engagements, awards etc...

After several months you may have made enough guest appearances to call yourself a seasoned radio guest.

Promos with some of your best reviews added to it are wonderful. Put the stars too. Need a graphic artist? Call me and I will make time to help you if humanly possible.

Your photos from book signings, events, awards and speaking engagements make great updated promos.

Celebrity endorsements are a nice bonus.

Collect and keep what you accomplish along the way and use it to keep momentum going for your book and hopefully create interest in your next one.

With book promotions there comes a time when offers can start coming your way and that is a beautiful feeling. Promoting a book is like pushing a boulder and then surprisingly it suddenly starts to roll in unexpected ways all by itself.

When invites are coming in, and people are discussing the book, you have done well.

When you are getting asked when your next book is coming out, you have done well.

When you get emails telling you that your book changed their life, you have done well.

18
KEEP YOUR EYES OPEN

"Learn the rules like a pro, so you can break them like an artist."
— Pablo Picasso

You are a magician or alchemist of sorts now, making something out of nothing. I love that. You see... once there was just an idea and then by applying your creative energy to that, a book was born. It's now something concrete and tangible that you can hold in your hands.

People in Japan, India, Australia, the UK, Canada, and India are reading your Kindle.

Yes someone in Japan knows your name... How cool is that?

So you literally had an idea and made something out of thin air and it brings you a passive income too.

Look around differently. Notice little coffee shops and historical sites you never saw before. See signs announcing events and festivals. Maybe the little old theater in your area that does plays now.

Wine bar... art gallery... look around as a magic maker finding places to connect with your community and make wonderful experiences happen, speak your message in front of an audience and maybe even sell a few books.

Best wishes today and always.

ABOUT THE AUTHOR
ANNETTE MUNNICH

Annette
Munnich

Annette Munnich is the owner of Stellium Books which is multi-genre publishing and publishing services since 2015. She was on Baltimore Talk Radio AM 680 as part of the SPEAK YOUR MIND Radio Show Saturday nights on WCBM.

Annette had her own successful paranormal radio show (Python Radio) for 4 years on three networks from 1997 to 2011 and enjoyed interviewing some of the biggest names in the field. She also worked behind the scenes for two radio stations for a total of 6 years.

Annette is an artist, graphic artist and a PR Specialist. She has designed more than 40 book covers, many of which became bestsellers, hot new releases, and 3 became number one bestsellers in their genres on Amazon. Annette has created posters, promos and professional pics for celebrities of television, movies and music. She has 3 pieces in the Museum of Contemporary Art.

She is the author of The Ghost Journal and Record Book, Nine Angels For Prosperity and Abundance and the illustrator for the Billy Rabbit Adventures Children's Book Series. She is a contributing author in Stellium Book's Best Selling Anthologies on Amazon, Amazing Paranormal Encounters Volumes 1-4. She is also a contributing author for Connections From The Hereafter.

Annette was born and raised in Chicago, Illinois and currently resides 30 miles south of the city. She has also lived in Texas, Ohio, Missouri and Oklahoma. She has 5 children and 5 grandchildren.

Stellium Books on FB
https://www.facebook.com/stelliumbooks/

Stellium Books Blog
Stellium Books For Readers and Writers
https://stelliumbooks.wordpress.com/2016/09/10/stelliu
m-books-for-readers-and-writers/

Website
www.stelliumbooks.com

Contact:
annette.munnich@gmail.com